THE ULTIMATE
DETROIT TIGERS
TRIVIA BOOK

A Collection of Amazing Trivia Quizzes
and Fun Facts for Die-Hard Tigers Fans!

Ray Walker

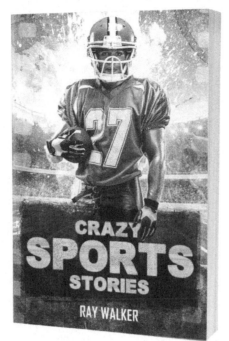

CONTENTS

INTRODUCTION

Obviously, you're inspired by your favorite team. In this case, the team in the spotlight is on none other than the Detroit Tigers, one of the original franchises in the American League. They are surely one of the best ever in the entire glorious history of Major League Baseball – although arch-rival Cleveland Indians fans might want to argue just a bit about that claim.

The city of Detroit, "the Motor City" or "Motown," has always been filled with winning pro teams: the inimitable Detroit Pistons ("The Bad Boys") and their three NBA championships, the Red Wings flying around the Joe Louis Arena or the new Little Caesars Arena ice, and the Detroit Lions in the NFL (never quite a powerhouse, but always featured in a national TV game on Thanksgiving Day).

But your Detroit Tigers are extra special. There's no place in the world to play hardball like their unique home stadium, Comerica Park in Downtown Detroit, filled with 41,297 screaming Detroiters.

Next year, the Detroit Tigers will celebrate 126 years of existence at (or near!) the peak of the baseball world, and you'll be there, armed with all the trivia and fun facts on their colorful players, big signings and trades, and the incredible emotional highs and lows of a world championship team. The Tigers have had more than their fair share of lows, and that doesn't mean just the arm problems of a few pitchers —but the decline of a city, and an entire region, as the world's car manufacturing capital. But we all must overcome, and there are many more merrier moments (like the last World Series win in 1984, along with near misses in 2013 and 2014).

Clearly, you may use the book as you wish. Each chapter contains twenty quiz questions that mix multiple-choice and true-or-false formats, an answer key (don't worry, it's on a separate page!), and a section of ten "Did You Know?" factoids about the team.

For the record, the information and stats in this book are current up to the beginning of 2020. The Tigers will surely break more records and win many more awards as the seasons march on, so keep this in mind when you're watching the next game with your friends. You never know: Someone could suddenly start a conversation with the phrase "Did you know…?" And you'll be ready.

CHAPTER 1:

ORIGINS & HISTORY

QUIZ TIME!

1. What was the name of the Tigers' first ballpark in 1894?

    a. Boulevard Park

    b. Broadway Park

    c. Comerica Park

    d. Detroit Arena

2. After only a year, they moved to a new park. Who was the Detroit owner at that time?

    a. Con Strouthers

    b. George Steinbrenner

    c. George Vanderbeck

    d. George Washington Carver

3. What was the military unit that originally gave the Tigers their name?

    a. Detroit Brigade

    b. Detroit Light Guard

    c. Flying Tiger Fleet

    d. Fighting Tiger Regiment

4. On April 28, 1896, the Tigers played their first Western League game. Who did they beat?

   a. Columbus Senators
   b. Grand Rapids Rippers
   c. Minneapolis Millers
   d. St. Paul Saints

5. When did the aforementioned Western League become the American League?

   a. 1897
   b. 1899
   c. 1900
   d. 1902

6. Who did the Tigers acquire in 1905 who's now considered among the best players ever?

   a. Frank Chance
   b. Ty Cobb
   c. Christy Mathewson
   d. Honus Wagner

7. After the Tigers won the AL pennant in 1907, who did they lose to in the Series?

   a. Boston Doves
   b. Chicago Cubs
   c. Pittsburgh Pirates
   d. Philadelphia Phillies

8. In their early years, how many times did the Tigers make it to the Series before finally winning in 1935?

a. 2

b. 3

c. 4

d. 6

9. The Tigers are the oldest continuous one-name, one-city franchise in the AL.

a. True

b. False

10. In which of the following years did Detroit NOT win the Series?

a. 1925

b. 1935

c. 1945

d. 1968

11. When the Tigers played in their new digs, Bennett Park, in 1896, what was that Detroit area called?

a. Corktown

b. Downtown

c. Motortown

d. Olde Towne

12. What was Detroit's best winning percentage ever, recorded in 1934?

a. .640

b. .652

c. .656

d. .685

13. On April 25, 1901, in their first American League game at home against Milwaukee, Detroit entered the 9th inning behind, 13-4. What was the final score?

    a. Milwaukee, 13-10
    b. Milwaukee, 13-12
    c. Detroit, 14-13
    d. Detroit, 16-13

14. When Ty Cobb joined the Tigers, which of the following players was NOT a teammate?

    a. Sam Crawford
    b. Bill Donovan
    c. Hughie Jennings
    d. Schoolboy Rowe

15. In 1912, a new stadium was built on the site of Bennett Park. Who was it named after?

    a. Businessman William Boeing
    b. Company owner Horace Dodge
    c. Inventor Elijah McCoy
    d. Team owner Frank Navin

16. Navin Field was later renamed Tigers Stadium. How many seasons did Detroit play in that venerable park?

    a. 66
    b. 77
    c. 88
    d. 99

17. Arguably the most famous Tiger ever, what was Ty Cobb's real first name?

    a. Tyrell
    b. Tyrone
    c. Tyrus
    d. Typhoon

18. Cobb's nickname reflected the fine state he came from. What was it?

    a. The Georgia Peach
    b. The Georgia Pecan
    c. The Tennessee Tornado
    d. The Texas Lone Star

19. Ty set a kit of MLB records in his career. How many, to be exact?

    a. 50
    b. 60
    c. 75
    d. 90

20. Detroit owner Frank Navin became "the most powerful man" in the AL after Ban Johnson's retirement. What was his first Tiger job?

    a. Bookkeeper
    b. Scorekeeper
    c. Scout
    d. Treasurer

QUIZ ANSWERS

1. A - Boulevard Park

2. C - George Vanderbeck

3. B - Detroit Light Guard

4. A - Columbus Senators

5. C - 1900

6. B - Ty Cobb

7. B - Chicago Cubs

8. C - 4

9. A - True

10. A - 1925

11. A - Corktown

12. C - .656

13. C - Detroit, 14-13

14. D - Schoolboy Rowe

15. D - Team owner Frank Navin

16. C - 88

17. C - Tyrus

18. A - The Georgia Peach

19. D - 90

20. A - Bookkeeper

DID YOU KNOW?

1. When the Tigers grabbed Cobb in 1905, he came from Augusta in the Sally League in exchange for pitcher Eddie Cicotte, $700 and an extra $50 for "immediate delivery."

2. Cobb destroyed more MLB records than any other player in history. In 1911, he batted .420, two points behind the all-time AL record of Nat Lajoie in 1901.

3. The 1912 season was "stained" because the Tigers players went on strike in support of Ty Cobb, who had been suspended for taking a swing at a New York fan.

4. That May 18 strike in 1912 forced the Tigers to field an amateur team against Philadelphia. The Tigers tiptoed off the field 24-2 losers.

5. In 1915, manager Hughie Jennings led Detroit to 100 victories. But he called it "the biggest disappointment" of his career, as the Red Sox and Babe Ruth finished first with 101 wins.

6. The 1934 season saw Detroit try to sign Babe Ruth as manager, but it couldn't do the deal. They settled on catcher Mickey Cochrane, and Schoolboy Rowe pitched a record 16 straight wins.

7. That same year, the Tigers couldn't sink the Cardinals in the World Series. Commissioner Kenesaw Mountain Landis had to personally remove St. Louis outfielder

Ducky Medwick in Game 7 under a shower of debris from Detroit fans.

8. The Tigers finally broke through to win their first Series in 1935. Cochrane's bravery on the basepaths versus the Cubs did the trick to win Game 6. Each player got a $6,544 share.

9. Owner Frank Navin finally witnessed his team on the victory podium in 1935. Suddenly in November, he developed a heart problem and died at 64.

10. Detroit dominated in 1940 to grab its sixth pennant. Despite winning twice in the World Series, Tigers pitcher Bobo Newsome lost the decisive seventh game as Detroit fell to Cincinnati.

CHAPTER 2:

WHAT'S IN A NAME?

QUIZ TIME!

1. Before there were the Tigers, Detroit had a baseball team named after the University of Michigan's mascot. What was it?

   a. Bears
   b. Cougars
   c. Wolverines
   d. Wombats

2. The name "Tigers" comes from a military group that fought with the ferocity of the jungle animal. Which was the first war they fought in?

   a. Civil War
   b. Mexican-American War
   c. Spanish-American War
   d. War of 1812

3. The reason Detroit wears blue, as well as tiger orange, has various explanations. Which of these is NOT one of them?

a. The most popular car color in Detroit's history is blue.

b. The Michigan Wolverines wear blue.

c. The Union Army wore blue in the Civil War.

4. In his book, St. Louis Cardinals great Bob Gibson takes fans through the first game of the historic 1968 World Series against Denny McLain and the Tigers. What's the title of the book?

a. Gibby vs. Mac

b. Out by Out

c. Pitch by Pitch

d. Stranger to the Game

5. Denny McLain was a bit eccentric, flying his own plane to games and entertaining friends by playing the organ. What was his full name?

a. Daniel Douglas McLain

b. David Denham McLain

c. Dennis Dale McLain

d. Dennis Delbert McLain

6. In that 1968 Series against the Cards, there was one Detroit player nicknamed "Mr. Tiger." Who was he?

a. Norm Cash

b. Bill Freehan

c. Willie Horton

d. Al Kaline

7. When he was a kid in Baltimore, Al Kaline developed an infection in his left foot and had to have two inches of bone removed. What's this condition's technical name?

a. bacterial meningitis

b. osteomyelitis

c. osteoporosis

d. otitis media

8. When Kaline signed with Detroit directly out of high school at 18, which group did join?

   a. "Bonanza Boy"

   b. "Bonus Baby"

   c. "Bonus Boy"

   d. "Manchild Millionaire"

9. The Tigers have had various nicknames. Which of these is NOT one?

   a. The Bengals

   b. The Motor City Kitties

   c. The Motor City Madmen

   d. The Tigs

10. Which of the following sluggers was referred to as "Big Daddy" in the '90s?

   a. Big Sam Thompson

   b. Cecil Fielder

   c. Lance Parrish

   d. Cletus Poffenberger

11. As Detroit honed in on the 1984 Series, which broadcaster coined the term, "Bless you boys!"?

   a. Al Ackerman

   b. Frank Beckmann

c. Ernie Harwell

d. Rick Rizzs

12. From 1938 to 1960, Detroit played in Briggs Stadium, named after manufacturer Walter Briggs Sr. Which business was he in?

   a. Car batteries

   b. Electrical

   c. Plumbing

   d. Wiring

13. In what World Series year did the rally cry, "Eat 'em up, Tigers! Eat 'em up!" become famous?

   a. 1935

   b. 1945

   c. 1968

   d. 1984

14. The Tigers rode the pitching strength of "Fire" Trucks in the '40s. What was his first name?

   a. Trey

   b. Valentine

   c. Victor

   d. Virgil

15. The Braves had Aaron, but the Tigers also had a "Hammerin' Hank." Who was he?

   a. Greenberg

   b. Hopp

   c. Manush

   d. McKain

16. Miguel Cabrera's heavy bat earned him a few nicknames. Which of these is NOT one?

    a. Big Cat
    b. Cabby
    c. King Kong Cabrera
    d. Miggy

17. Al Kaline may have the record for most Detroit nicknames. Besides Mr. Tiger, which of these is NOT one?

    a. Big Al
    b. The Line
    c. Salty
    d. Salt in Your Wounds

18. The Detroit mascot is named after one specific part of Tiger anatomy. What is it?

    a. Claws
    b. Eyes
    c. Paws
    d. Tails

19. Pitcher Hal Newhouser was treated royally by the Tigers during his reign from 1939 to 1955. What was his nickname?

    a. Count Houser
    b. King Hal
    c. Newhouser the Knight
    d. Prince Hal

20. Schoolboy Rowe hurled for Tiger World Series teams in 1934, 1935, and 1940. What was his first name?

a. Carl

b. Lynwood

c. Roger

d. Samuel

QUIZ ANSWERS

1. C - Wolverine
2. A - Civil War
3. A - The most popular car color in Detroit's history is blue.
4. C - *Pitch by Pitch*, subtitled "My View of One Unforgettable Game"
5. C - Dennis Dale McLain
6. D - Al Kaline
7. B - osteomyelitis
8. B - "bonus baby"
9. C - Motor City Madmen
10. B - Cecil Fielder
11. A - Al Ackerman
12. C - Plumbing
13. C - 1968
14. D - Virgil
15. A - Greenberg
16. C - King Kong Cabrera
17. D - Salt in Your Wounds
18. C - Paws
19. D - Prince Hal
20. B - Lynwood

DID YOU KNOW?

1. Rowe received his nickname "Schoolboy" because he was a 15-year-old student playing on a men's team in Arkansas.

2. Schoolboy battled against the St. Louis Gashouse Gang in the 1934 World Series. In Game 2, he recorded a 12-inning complete-game win. Despite another complete game in Game 6, he lost to the Cards' Paul "Daffy" Dean.

3. During his 16-game win streak, Schoolboy revealed his secret: "Just eat a lot of vittles, climb on that mound, wrap my fingers around the ball and say to it, 'Edna, honey, let's go!'" Edna was his high school sweetheart.

4. Detroit had a first baseman named Lu Blue in the 1920s. He was the only player in MLB history with the first name "Luzerne."

5. Tito Fuentes played second base for Detroit for a mere year in 1977. Certainly, his nickname rolled off the tongue a bit better than his real name, "Rigoberto."

6. Coot Veal (real name: Orville Inman Veal) broke in with Detroit in 1958 and battled Billy Martin, future Yankee manager, for playing time.

7. Skeeter Barnes came to Detroit at age 34 in 1991 and served time as a utility infielder. His mom gave William the nickname but never explained why.

8. Six feet, three inches and 215 pounds, William Chester Jacobson became better known as "Baby Doll" in 1915.

9. Shaky Joe Grzenda pitched for the Tigers in 1961. His pitching was shaky and he drank two pots of coffee a day while chain-smoking.

10. Matt Tuiasosopo was a backup outfielder for the Tigers in 2013. His dad Manu had made a bigger splash in the NFL in the 1980s.

CHAPTER 3:

FAMOUS QUOTES

QUIZ TIME!

1. Brooks Robinson called one Tigers player "the epitome of what a great outfielder is all about." Who was the man?

   a. Hank Greenberg
   b. Harry Heilmann
   c. Willie Horton
   d. Al Kaline

2. Kaline turned right around and lauded another player: "The number one right-handed hitter I've ever seen." Who was the Tiger?

   a. Miguel Cabrera
   b. Ty Cobb
   c. Charlie Gehringer
   d. Bobby Veach

3. Lefty Gomez joked about Tigers great Charlie Gehringer: "Charlie Gehringer's in a ___. He bats .350 and stays there all season." What's the missing word?

a. groove

b. rut

c. slump

d. tunnel

4. A famous Tigers pitcher said the following: "When you're a winner, you're always happy, but if you're happy as a loser, you'll always be a loser." Who was he?

    a. Mark "The Bird" Fidrych

    b. Willie Hernández

    c. Mickey Lolich

    d. Jack Morris

5. What did Mark Teixeira say was impressive about Justin Verlander?

    a. "He's pretty incredible. He's throwing 100 mph in the 8th inning."

    b. "He's pretty fast. He's throwing faster than any pitcher alive."

    c. "He's got good velocity—better than any pitcher in history."

    d. "He's got good stuff. You might as well wear a blindfold."

6. What word's missing from the following Ty Cobb quote: "When I began playing the game, baseball was about as sentimental as a kick in the _____"?

    a. butt

    b. crotch

    c. rear

    d. tail

7. Which player showed up in a stretch limo during the 1994 baseball strike, and quipped, "I'm rich—what am I supposed to do—hide it?"

   a. Storm Davis
   b. Junior Felix
   c. Travis Fryman
   d. Sweet Lou Whitaker

8. When Red Sox slugger Ted Williams spoke in awe of Virgil "Fire" Trucks, he claimed, "He threw as hard as _____," Who was the other flame-thrower?

   a. (Spud) Chandler
   b. (Bob) Feller
   c. (Tex) Hughson
   d. (Dizzy) Trout

9. What did Andy Van Slyke say when asked how it was to play for Detroit manager Jim Leyland?

   a. "It's never dull, it's always smoky."
   b. "It's like a merry-go-round."
   c. "It's more fun than an all-night poker party."
   d. "It's basically a barrel of laughs."

10. Detroit GM Jim Campbell once cracked, "After I made that trade, I tossed my roll of Tums into a trash basket on the corner." Who was the Tiger traded?

   a. Lou Boudreau
   b. Denny McLain
   c. Mickey Lolich
   d. Johnny Sain

11. What word's missing from Sparky Anderson's take on his own job: "A baseball manager is a necessary ____"?

    a. evil
    b. guy
    c. hero
    d. luxury

12. How would you complete Sparky's quote? "Me carrying a briefcase is like…"

    a. A hotdog wearing earrings
    b. A snowball's chance in hell
    c. A sunny day in April in Detroit
    d. A top Tiger team playing in front of no fans

13. What was the second part of Sparky's formula for players? "Players have two things to do: Play and…"

    a. keep out of trouble
    b. keep their mouths shut
    c. listen to their manager
    d. score more than the opponent

14. What did Ty Cobb refer to his "ball bat" as?

    a. A wonderful tool
    b. A wondrous weapon
    c. A worrisome weapon
    d. A wizard's wand

15. Cobb was brilliant with the bat himself, but about whom did he say the following: "He was the finest natural hitter in the history of the game."?

a. Babe Ruth

b. Stan Musial

c. Shoeless Joe Jackson

d. The Headless Horseman

16. Denny McLain showed some jealousy toward his teammate Mickey Lolich, winner of three games in the '68 Series. He snorted, "I wouldn't trade one _____ for 12 Mickey Loliches." Who was the one?

a. Bob Gibson

b. Tom Seaver

c. Luis Tiant

d. Wilbur Wood

17. During the 1967 Detroit race riots, one Tiger tried to help bring peace. "I was blessed I was involved in that because it made me a better person and human being," he said. Who was this hero?

a. Gates Brown

b. Lenny Green

c. Willie Horton

d. Earl Wilson

18. What did Ralph Houk do in winter when there was no baseball?

a. "I hibernate until the first pitch is thrown."

b. "I hit the books until the hitters come back."

c. "I sleep an awful lot and dream of baseball."

d. "I stare out the window and wait for spring."

19. Wahoo Sam Crawford was a turn-of-the-century Tiger. Why didn't he like telephones?

   a. "Anybody wants to talk to you, they can come to see you."
   b. "Back in the day, receiving a love letter was more interesting."
   c. "I don't like to talk that much."
   d. "Telephones are the future. All I need is a bat and ball."

20. Who was Tiger manager Hughie Jennings talking about when he said: "No other player ever crowded so many remarkable accomplishments into such a short time"?

   a. Ty Cobb
   b. Frank Huelsman
   c. Topper Rigney
   d. Louis Sockalexis

QUIZ ANSWERS

1. D - Al Kaline

2. A - Miguel Cabrera

3. B - rut

4. A - Mark "The Bird" Fidrych

5. A - "He's pretty incredible. He's throwing 100 mph in the 8th inning."

6. B - crotch

7. D - Sweet Lou Whitaker

8. B - Bob Feller

9. A - "It's never dull, it's always smoky."

10. B - Denny McLain

11. A - evil

12. A - A hotdog wearing earrings

13. B - keep their mouths shut

14. B - A wondrous weapon

15. C - Shoeless Joe Jackson

16. A - Bob Gibson

17. C - Willie Horton

18. D - "I stare out the window and wait for spring."

19. A - "Anybody wants to talk to you, they can come to see you."

20. D - Louis Sockalexis

DID YOU KNOW?

1. Long-time Tiger announcer Al Ackerman said the following about Sparky Anderson: "Sparky came here two years ago promising to build a team in his own image. Now the club is looking for small white-haired infielders with .212 batting averages."

2. Mark Fidrych worked hard on the mound, but not so much at home: "Sometimes I get lazy and let the dishes stack up. But they don't stack too high. I've only got four dishes."

3. "The Bird" Fidrych also commented on the dilemma faced by some players: "I'm supposed to be writing a book and I can hardly read."

4. Mickey Lolich helped a few fans by saying, "I guess you could say I'm the redemption of the fat guy. A guy will be watching me on TV and see that I don't look in any better shape than he is. 'Hey Maude,' he'll holler. 'Get a load of this guy. And he's a 20-game winner.'"

5. Why could Norm Cash crush the ball so? "I owe my success to expansion pitching, a short right field fence, and my hollow bats."

6. Getting to the big leagues was even tough on Al Kaline: "I'll never forget that first night with the team. Going to the ballpark on the bus was the hardest 30 minutes of my

life. I had to walk down that aisle between all the players. I really didn't know too much about the Detroit Tigers at that time."

7. Being a big leaguer isn't all happiness either, according to Kaline: "It hurt me a great deal. It put a lot of pressure on me because I was at a young age and the writers around here and throughout the league started comparing me to Cobb."

8. Besides tons of controversy and links to the Mob, Denny McLain was a simple guy: "All that running and exercise can do for you is make you healthy."

9. Jack Morris clarified he didn't want to be interviewed by a female when he was just out of the shower: "The only time I talk to a woman when I'm naked is when she's on top of me or I'm on top of her."

10. Kirk Gibson showed one reason he was an exemplary Tiger: "I have faced many different obstacles in my life, and have always maintained a strong belief that no matter the circumstances, I could overcome those obstacles."

CHAPTER 4:

TIGERS RECORDS

QUIZ TIME!

1. In its approximately 120 years of existence as of the beginning of the 2020 season, what's Detroit's winning percentage?

   a. .492

   b. .500

   c. .504

   d. .524

2. How many AL pennants has Detroit snagged during that time?

   a. 7

   b. 9

   c. 11

   d. 14

3. Who is the winningest manager in Tigers history?

   a. Sparky Anderson

   b. Brad Ausmus

    c. Ron Gardenhire

    d. Jim Leyland

4. Which of the following Detroit players has NOT had his number retired?

    a. Kirk Gibson

    b. Willie Horton

    c. Hal Newhouser

    d. Alan Trammel

5. Besides the usual batting suspects, who's the all-time Tigers leader in strikeouts?

    a. Miguel Cabrera

    b. Norm Cash

    c. Brandon Inge

    d. Lou Whitaker

6. Ty Cobb broke about every conceivable Tigers batting record. Which of these did he NOT break?

    a. Doubles

    b. Homers

    c. Total bases

    d. Triples

7. The subject of sacrifice hits brings up a new name. Who is the Tigers' career record-holder?

    a. Donie Bush

    b. Charley O'Leary

    c. Bobby Veach

    d. Ossie Vitt

8. The Tigers had some toughies take pitches over the years. Who's the hit-by-pitch leader?

   a. Damion Easley
   b. Bill Freehan
   c. Al Kaline
   d. Chet Lemon

9. When this hitter came up, you knew a dinger was very likely. Who's the Detroit leader in at-bats per home run?

   a. Rocky Colavito
   b. Cecil Fielder
   c. Dean Palmer
   d. Marcus Thames

10. Hooks Dauss happens to have the most wins of any Tiger pitcher. How many?

   a. 198
   b. 214
   c. 223
   d. 236

11. Which of the following Detroit hurlers has the best win-loss percentage?

   a. Doug Fister
   b. Aurélio Lopez
   c. Max Scherzer
   d. Ed Summers

12. Which of these pitchers appeared in more games on the mound than any other Tiger?

    a. Tommy Bridges
    b. John Hiller
    c. George Mullin
    d. Dizzy Trout

13. In terms of hitting, Ty Cobb was it. What's his MLB-best career batting average?

    a. .344
    b. .355
    c. .366
    d. .377

14. When Hammerin' Hank Greenberg batted in 184 runs in 1937, he led the American League but fell short of the single-season record. Who was better?

    a. Jimmie Foxx
    b. Chuck Klein
    c. Babe Ruth
    d. Hack Wilson

15. On a single September day in 1908, Ed Summers did something almost unheard of. What was his feat?

    a. He struck out 30 in two games.
    b. He homered five times.
    c. He pitched two complete-game wins.
    d. He pitched two shutouts.

16. In 1904, George Mullin pitched 42 complete games. What's more amazing is how many starts he did it in. Can you guess?

    a. 44
    b. 48
    c. 50
    d. 54

17. The largest opening day crowd ever on April 6, 1971, was 54,089. Who was the opponent?

    a. Boston
    b. Cleveland
    c. Minnesota
    d. New York Yankees

18. The magical 1984 season saw Detroit rack up 104 wins. Who was the victim in that year's World Series?

    a. Atlanta
    b. Houston
    c. Los Angeles
    d. San Diego

19. 2003 wasn't such a good year for Detroit. What was the record number of losses that piled up?

    a. 114
    b. 119
    c. 122
    d. 126

20. José "Papa Grande" Valverde set a Tiger single-season record in 2011 that still stands. What is it?

a. 45 games started

b. 49 saves

c. 9 shutouts

d. 308 strikeouts

QUIZ ANSWERS

1. C - .504

2. C - 11

3. A - Sparky Anderson

4. A - Kirk Gibson

5. C - Brandon Inge

6. B - Homers

7. A - Donie Bush

8. B - Bill Freehan

9. D - Marcus Thames

10. C - 223

11. C - Max Scherzer

12. B - John Hiller

13. C - .366

14. D - Hack Wilson

15. C - He pitched two complete-game wins.

16. A - 44

17. B - Cleveland

18. D - San Diego

19. B - 119

20. B - 49 saves

DID YOU KNOW?

1. In the first half of the 2010 season, Valverde sported a 0.94 ERA while breaking another Tiger record by pitching 24 straight scoreless innings.

2. Before heading to the Nats, Max Scherzer became the first Tiger pitcher to ever start the season 12-0 in 2013. George Mullin began 1909 with an 11-0 mark.

3. Although Arizona's Randy Johnson won three games in one World Series in 2001, Detroit's Mickey Lolich is the only lefthander ever with three complete-game wins in a Series (1968).

4. Lolich also owns the Tigers single-season strikeout score with 308.

5. In 1953, Harvey Kuenn batted 679 times, which was the Tigers record until 2014 when Ian Kinsley broke it. He also dropkicked a 53-yard field goal as a teen football player in Wisconsin.

6. Hank Greenberg bashed records with his bat and was also the first Jewish superstar in MLB. In 1934, he had Detroit fans on edge while he decided whether or not to play on major Jewish holidays.

7. "Hankus Pankus" or "the Hebrew Hammer" Greenberg was also one of the first white opponents to openly welcome African-American Jackie Robinson in 1947.

8. "Wahoo Sam" Crawford came from Wahoo, Nebraska. He still holds the MLB record of 309 career triples. He was also teammates and intense rivals with terrifying Ty Cobb.

9. Roy Cullenbine had the uncanny ability to walk and once drew bases on balls in a record 22 consecutive games. In his career, he had almost as many walks (853) as hits (1,072).

10. Jimmy Bloodworth grounded into the most Tiger double plays (29) ever in 1943. He got his upper body strength dragging boats across Apalachicola Bay in Florida as a youngster.

CHAPTER 5:

HOW ABOUT A TRADE?

QUIZ TIME!

1. Detroit GM Dave Dombrowski "got crushed" due to his 2013 trade for Robbie Ray who lasted only a year before being shipped out. What fan favorite was sent packing for Ray?

   a. Matthew Boyd
   b. Doug Fister
   c. Austin Jackson
   d. Max Scherzer

2. In 2014, Detroit sent two players to Cincy for Alfredo Simon who turned out to be a bust. Which of the former two blossomed as a Red?

   a. Joba Chamberlain
   b. Rajai Davis
   c. Dixon Machado
   d. Eugenio Suarez

3. Who was the Detroit executive responsible for most trades in 2019?

    a. Al Avila
    b. Christopher Ilitch
    c. Bo Schembechler
    d. Jack Zeller

4. Chad Green and Luis Cessa were sent to the Yankees for one player in 2015. Then that player was flipped for Jeimer Candelario and Isaac Paredes in 2017. Who was he?

    a. Shane Green
    b. Mark Lowe
    c. Drew VerHagen
    d. Justin Wilson

5. Of the three players traded for J.D. Martínez in 2017, Dawel Lugo is the only one to appear at the big-league level. How many strikeouts does he have along with his 87 hits?

    a. 89
    b. 87
    c. 79
    d. 65

6. 2017 saw Detroit trade Justin Upton to L.A. for Grayson Long and Elvin Rodríguez. For whom did Long recently make his last appearance?

    a. Erie SeaWolves
    b. Mississippi Braves

c. Reno Aces

d. Visalia Rawhide

7. After Justin Verlander was traded away following 13 years as Detroit's best pitcher, he became even more dominant. For which team?

a. Baltimore

b. Houston

c. Miami

d. San Francisco

8. The so-called centerpiece in the Verlander trade was Franklin Perez. How many starts does he have in the last two years in the minor leagues?

a. 9

b. 25

c. 46

d. 61

9. What's one word that writers use to describe what Detroit did to the Rangers when they got Ian Kinsler for Prince Fielder in 2013?

a. faked

b. fleeced

c. juiced

d. cheated

10. Which player became the face of the franchise after he was acquired from Miami in 2007?

a. Miguel Cabrera

b. Mike Hessman

c. Iván Rodríguez

d. Joel Zumaya

11. In 2004, who did Detroit trade for who turned into a three-time All-Star in the Motor City?

    a. Juan González
    b. Carlos Guillén
    c. Cameron Maybin
    d. Ramón Santiago

12. The Tigers were ready for a World Series run in 1984. What position did Willie Hernández fill when he came in a trade with Philly?

    a. Pinch hitter
    b. Pinch-runner
    c. Relief pitcher
    d. Starting pitcher

13. Detroit traded Steve Kemp for Chet Lemon in 1981. Afterward, Kemp bounced around baseball and was done by 1988. How many good years did Chet give Detroit?

    a. 5
    b. 7
    c. 9
    d. 11

14. Just after Harvey Kuenn won the batting title in 1959, he was traded to the rival Indians. For whom?

    a. Rocky Colavito
    b. Mudcat Grant

c. Jack Harshman

d. Morrie Martin

15. The Tigers dealt with Seattle to acquire Doug Fister and his 3-12 record in 2011. He promptly went 8-1 and Detroit won its first division crown in how many years?

a. 16

b. 20

c. 24

d. 28

16. Only days before getting Colavito, Detroit dealt with Cleveland for Norm Cash, who ended up playing 15 years and winning a World Series in Motown. Who went to the Indians?

a. Pete Burnside

b. Steve Demeter

c. Paul Foytack

d. Lou Skizas

17. In the '68 Series, the more illustrious Detroit pitchers Lolich and McLain were accompanied by another lights-out hurler, Earl Wilson. Which team traded him?

a. Baltimore

b. Boston

c. California

d. Oakland

18. The Tigers acquired Texas slugger Juan González in 1999. What was his nickname?

a. Juan Gone

b. Juan Get Your Gun

c. Going Going González

d. King Gone

19. Which ace grew up a stone's throw from Tigers Stadium and rooted for Detroit, but was traded away in 1987 before tossing a single Tiger pitch?

a. Doyle Alexander

b. Tom Glavine

c. Orel Hershiser

d. John Smoltz

20. What nickname did former Tiger GM Dave Dombrowski earn because of his penchant for making trades?

a. Dave the Dealer

b. Deal Me In Dave

c. Discount Dave

d. Trader Dave

QUIZ ANSWERS

1. B - Doug Fister

2. D - Eugenio Suarez

3. A - Al Avila

4. D - Justin Wilson

5. C - 79

6. A - Erie SeaWolves

7. B - Houston

8. A - 9

9. B - "fleeced"

10. A - Miguel Cabrera

11. B - Carlos Guillén

12. C - Relief pitcher

13. C - 9

14. A - Rocky Colavito

15. C - 24

16. B - Steve Demeter

17. B - Boston

18. A - Juan Gone

19. D - John Smoltz

20. D - Trader Dave

DID YOU KNOW?

1. Detroit traded for a better second baseman and pitching help just before the 2012 deadline. They brought in Omar Infante and Anibal Sanchez and gave up three guys who didn't pan out for Miami.

2. When they traded for Willie Hernández just before the magical '84 campaign, little did Detroit know that he'd end up winning the AL Cy Young and MVP Awards.

3. In 2019, the Tigers were looking to make some blockbuster moves because of what pundits called a "pitching-heavy" farm system.

4. When Detroit traded Harvey Kuenn to Cleveland for Rocky Colavito 60 years ago, fans of both teams were shocked. Detroit benefited more because Kuenn spent only a year in Cleveland before being shipped to the Giants.

5. After four productive years in Detroit, Rocky rejoined Cleveland in 1965. He then played in all 162 games in the outfield without a single error – an AL record.

6. "Trader Dave" Dombrowski has quite a rep for pulling the trade trigger. He was the Expos' GM from 1988 to 1991, the Marlins' GM from 1992 to 2001, and Detroit's GM from 2002 to 2015.

7. Acquiring David Price at the 2014 deadline, Dombrowski quipped: "Today it's great, it's nice, it's fine. I love to have

David Price. If we win, then I'll be very satisfied." They lost the ALDS to Baltimore.

8. When Dombrowski tried to pry Fister from the M's, he went into "junior high boyfriend mode," calling his Seattle counterpart Jack Zduriencik two or three times a day. He got his man.

9. Tigers GM Jim Campbell tired of World Series hero Willie Horton's contract demands in 1977. He went on to play for the Rangers, Indians, Blue Jays, A's and Mariners.

10. Fans cried when favorite Curtis Granderson was traded to the Yankees. But Detroit made out with Phil Coke, Austin Jackson, Max Scherzer and Dan Schlereth in the three-team trade.

CHAPTER 6:

CHAT ABOUT STATS

QUIZ TIME!

1. Ty Cobb took the field as a Tiger for the first time on August 30, 1905. How many games did he play for Detroit?

    a. 2,694
    b. 2,877
    c. 3,033
    d. 3,152

2. The 1945 season ended strangely with Washington sitting by as Detroit edged them for the pennant. Why did the Senators finish a week early?

    a. They made their park available for pro football.
    b. They made their park available for military parades.
    c. They made their park available for political rallies.
    d. They made their park available as a field hospital.

3. Behind Hall-of-Famer George Kell in 1950, Detroit fell three games short. How long had they led the league that year?

a. 92 days

b. 105 days

c. 119 days

d. 136 days

4. Which Tiger became the youngest ever to cop the batting title in 1955?

a. Babe Birrer

b. Van Fletcher

c. Al Kaline

d. Chick King

5. Walter Briggs Jr. ran the Tigers four years before selling the family stock to a syndicate of 11 radio and TV execs in 1956. Who eventually bought out his partners to own the team outright?

a. Kenyon Brown

b. John Fetzer

c. Fred Knorr

d. Muddy Ruel

6. When the 1968 squad took the lead on May 10, they never relinquished it. Who was the Tiger skipper that year?

a. Sparky Anderson

b. Jim Leyland

c. Mayo Smith

d. George Stallings

7. The '68 team was really dominant. How many games ahead of Baltimore did they finish?

a. 8

b. 12

c. 16

d. 19

8. Denny McLain's season was beyond belief, with a 31-6 record. Who was the previous pitcher to reach 30 wins in 1934?

    a. Lefty Grove

    b. Mel Harder

    c. Carl "The Meal Ticket" Hubbell

    d. Red Ruffing

9. After divisional play started in 1969, when was the first year Detroit won the AL East?

    a. 1970

    b. 1971

    c. 1972

    d. 1973

10. Who was the manager when Detroit snagged its first AL East crown?

    a. Yogi Berra

    b. Del Crandall

    c. Billy Martin

    d. Salty Parker

11. The late '70s saw the Tigers' middle infield combo, Alan Trammell and Lou Whitaker, in action. How many games did they play together?

a. 1,779

b. 1,825

c. 1,918

d. 1,999

12. In 1979, Sparky Anderson took over as Detroit's manager. He proceeded to win the division twice and the World Series once. How many years was he at the helm?

a. 12

b. 14

c. 16

d. 18

13. The 1984 season looked good from the start. What was Detroit's record in their first 40 games?

a. 32-8

b. 35-5

c. 37-3

d. 39-1

14. That year, Detroit led wire to wire, and won the World Series. What team had previously performed the same feat?

a. 1955 Dodgers

b. 1966 Orioles

c. 1975 Reds

d. 1979 Pirates

15. The 1987 campaign came down to the last day, and Detroit needed a win against Toronto to clinch. Which ace recorded a 1-0 shutout that day?

a. Doyle Alexander

b. Dickie Noles

c. Nate Snell

d. Frank Tanana

16. In 1995, Detroit brought in new brass focused on developing homegrown talent. Which of the following did NOT come up through the Tigers system?

a. Tony Clark

b. Juan Encarnación

c. Dwayne Henry

d. Brian Moehler

17. September 27, 1999, witnessed the last game at glorious Tiger Stadium. How many years had Detroit played there?

a. 77

b. 82

c. 87

d. 95

18. Fans wiped tears from their eyes before that final 1999 contest. How many former Tigers greats took the field in celebration?

a. 52

b. 63

c. 83

d. 99

19. Comerica Park hosted a Tigers' game for the first time on April 11, 2000. What was the temperature on that brisk day of baseball?

a. 30 degrees F.

b. 34 degrees F.

c. 38 degrees F.

d. 42 degrees F.

20. In 2004, Detroit drove to its best start since 1985. Which player that other teams had passed on became the new face of the Tigers?

a. Carlos Guillén

b. Nate Robinson

c. Iván "Pudge" Rodríguez

d. Andrés Torres

QUIZ ANSWERS

1. C - 3,033

2. A - They made their park available for pro football.

3. C - 119 days

4. C - Al Kaline

5. B - John Fetzer

6. C - Mayo Smith

7. B - 12

8. A - Lefty Grove

9. C - 1972

10. C - Billy Martin

11. C - 1,918

12. C - 16

13. B - 35-5

14. A - 1955 Dodgers

15. D - Frank Tanana

16. C - Dwayne Henry

17. C - 87

18. B - 63

19. B - 34 degrees F.

20. C - Iván "Pudge" Rodríguez

DID YOU KNOW?

1. "Pudge" Rodríguez, who played in the 2006 World Series with Detroit, is the Major Leagues leader in putouts by a catcher. He passed another "Pudge," Carlton Fisk when he caught his 2,227th game in 2009.

2. In 2006, the Tigers boasted one of the biggest turnarounds in franchise history. They notched 95 wins compared to a measly 43 in 2003.

3. The miraculous 2006 run ended in defeat to the Cardinals, in part due to five errors by Tiger pitchers.

4. In 2007, hurler Justin Verlander squashed the notion of a "sophomore slump" by going 18-6 with more than 200 innings and a no-hitter.

5. Curtis Granderson came alive in 2007 as the first player since Willie Mays to have 20 homers, 20 doubles, 20 triples and 20 stolen bases.

6. That very same year, Tiger second baseman Plácido Polanco played 141 error-free games to extend his larger streak to 186 errorless games.

7. Detroit's Magglio Ordonez hit the lights out in 2007 as well: a .363 BA, 216 hits, 54 doubles and 139 RBIs.

8. Detroit's 2009 version rode Verlander's 19 wins and 269 strikeouts, the best since Jack Morris. The season ended in

heartbreak with a tie-breaking loss to the Twins in the 163rd game.

9. 2010 was a roller-coaster ride with a dubious call denying Armando Gallaraga Detroit's first-ever perfect game. Rookie Austin Jackson jacked the ball with 181 hits, 34 doubles and 10 triples.

10. Verlander had one of the best seasons in 25 years in 2011 when he racked up 24 wins, a 2.40 ERA and 250 strikeouts to become the first Tigers pitcher to win the pitching Triple Crown since Hal Newhouser.

CHAPTER 7:

DRAFT DAY

QUIZ TIME!

1. In its history, Detroit has drafted 63 players in the first round of the MLB's Amateur Draft. Have any of them made it to the Hall of Fame?

   a. Yes
   b. No

2. One player, nicknamed "Tony the Tiger," was drafted Number 2 overall in the 1990 draft. What was his last name?

   a. Clark
   b. Giarratano
   c. Gwynn
   d. Hernández

3. Travis Fryman became a Tiger as a result of the 1987 draft. What was his hometown?

   a. Miami
   b. Pensacola

c. Tallahassee

d. Tampa

4. Kirk Gibson was drafted in 1978. Which of the following jobs did he NOT have with the Tigers after his playing career?

a. Broadcaster

b. Hitting coach

c. Bench coach

d. Pitching coach

5. Justin Verlander was drafted second overall in 2004. What was his university mascot at Old Dominion?

a. Bisons

b. Hokie Birds

c. Monarchs

d. Rams

6. One of the best catchers in MLB history, Lance Parrish, was drafted by Detroit at a different position. What was it?

a. First base

b. Outfield

c. Shortstop

d. Third base

7. Detroit draftee Parrish was a key cog in the 1984 championship team. Whose no-hitter did he catch that year?

a. Juan Berenguer

b. Sid Monge

c. Jack Morris

d. Dan Petry

8. After Lance "Big Wheel" Parrish retired, which team did he recently manage?

    a. Lakeland Flying Tigers

    b. Norwich Sea Unicorns

    c. West Michigan Whitecaps

    d. Vancouver Whitecaps

9. Seth Greisinger was the 6th overall pick in 1996. He missed the 2000 and 2001 seasons due to injury. How many games did he pitch for Detroit in 2002?

    a. 5

    b. 8

    c. 11

    d. 16

10. The Tigers used the first pick in 1997 to select Rice University's fastballer, Matt Anderson. Where did he end up when he pitched his last game in 2005?

    a. Boston

    b. Colorado

    c. San Diego

    d. Seattle

11. Cameron Maybin was Detroit's 2005 first-round pick and was then used as trade bait to bring in Miguel Cabrera. How many teams did he play for before returning to Detroit in 2016?

a. 2

b. 3

c. 4

d. 5

12. Eric Munson, drafted in 1999, spent five seasons in Tigerland. In which category did he finish in the top-5 among AL third basemen in 2003 and 2004

   a. Errors

   b. Hits

   c. Strikeouts

   d. Walks

13. Picked in 2006, Andrew Miller was also dangled to snag Cabrera. What state did he hail from?

   a. Georgia

   b. Florida

   c. South Carolina

   d. South Dakota

14. Matt Wheatland was picked at No. 8 overall in 2000. Did he ever appear in a Tigers game?

   a. Yes

   b. No

15. One of the reasons Wheatland was picked by Detroit was the speed of his fastball in high school. What was it?

   a. 90 mph

   b. 92 mph

   c. 95 mph

   d. 98 mph

16. Nick Castellanos was picked 44th overall with a supplementary first-round choice in 2010. What special game did he play in during the 2012 season?

    a. All-Star Futures Game
    b. All-Star Game
    c. ALDS, Game 1
    d. World Series, Game 1

17. Detroit took Kenny Baugh with the 11th overall pick in the 2001 draft. Which of the following team did NOT draft Baugh previously?

    a. Minnesota
    b. Oakland
    c. Tampa Bay

18. Catcher James Thomas McCann was drafted by Detroit in the second round in 2011. What nickname did he earn for his strong arm?

    a. Cannon McCann
    b. McCannon
    c. The McCann Gun
    d. Machine Gun McCann

19. Pitcher Kyle Sleeth was Detroit's third overall pick in 2003. What surgery cut his career short?

    a. Ankle
    b. Knee
    c. Shoulder
    d. Tommy John

20. Scott Moore was Detroit's first-round selection in 2002. Yet he didn't make a mark in Detroit, Chicago, Baltimore, or Houston. How many games did he play altogether for these teams?

    a. 120
    b. 152
    c. 161
    d. 175

QUIZ ANSWERS

1. B - No

2. A - Tony Clark

3. B - Pensacola

4. D - Pitching coach

5. C - Monarchs

6. D - Third base

7. C - Jack Morris

8. C - West Michigan Whitecaps

9. B - 8

10. B - Colorado

11. B - 3

12. A - Errors

13. B - Florida

14. B - No

15. C - 95 mph

16. A - All-Star Futures Game

17. A - Minnesota

18. B - McCannon

19. D - Tommy John

20. B - 152

DID YOU KNOW?

1. The Tigers passed on left-handers to pick righty Jacob Turner in 2009. He stands 6' 5", weighs 210, and hums the ball like Rick Porcello and Justin Verlander. After appearing in six games in two seasons, he was traded to Miami.

2. GM Dave Dombrowski's draft strategy has always been to pick the best pitcher available, but everybody knows prospects are unknown commodities until proven in the big leagues.

3. When Detroit draftee Casey Mize was said to have "a high floor," it meant he might not become a star, but he'd be a solid starting pitcher if he stayed healthy.

4. Detroit had success with Jack Morris and Lou Whitaker, both drafted in the fifth round. Coming in the fifth also, Alex Avila's family connections helped. He went on to play in 760 games for the Tigers.

5. George "Buck" Farmer struck out 22 Dacula (Georgia) High School batters in 2008. Missing out on the Braves in 2009 by heading to Georgia Tech, Detroit grabbed Buck in 2013 and he filled a bullpen role.

6. The 1975 and 1976 draft classes yielded results for Detroit. Alan Trammell, Jason Thompson and Dan Petry became top Tigers contributors.

7. Brandon Inge was drafted in 1998 and played 12 years for Detroit. One writer called him a "super-utility dervish."

8. Glenn Wilson, picked by Detroit in 1980, was traded for Willie Hernández just before the historic 1984 season. The other player used to entice Willie and Dave Bergman was John Wockenfuss.

9. Christin Stewart was Detroit's compensatory pick in 2015 after losing Max Scherzer in free agency. Stewart was listed with "above-average bat speed that translated into plus raw power."

10. The Tigers used the No. 1 pick in 2020 to grab Spencer Torkelson from Arizona State. Like some before, he's been called "the total package."

CHAPTER 8:

PITCHER & CATCHER TIDBITS

QUIZ TIME!

1. Tigers great Hal Newhouser took advantage of the talent drop due to World War II to dominate in 1944 and `45. What did he almost pull off in 1946?

   a. His third straight Cy Young
   b. His third straight ERA title
   c. His third straight HR title
   d. His third straight MVP

2. In fact, Newhouser tried to enlist to serve in World War II, but was turned down because of a "heart problem."

   a. True
   b. False

3. Who was Newhouser's batterymate and future manager that returned as a war-time fill-in at 35 years old after eight years out of the game?

   a. Mickey Cochrane
   b. Bill Freehan

c. Paul Richards

d. Birdie Tebbetts

4. Which Tigers pitcher holds the club's all-time ERA mark of 2.34?

a. Harry Coveleski

b. Bill Donovan

c. Ed Killian

d. Ed Summers

5. Which pitcher and his wicked curveball won Game 6 against the Cubs in the 1935 World Series, gifting the Motor City its first MLB championship?

a. Elden Auker

b. Tommy Bridges

c. Alvin Crowder

d. Schoolboy Rowe

6. After playing on all four World Series teams for Detroit between 1930 and 1946, Bridges finished up with a no-hitter in the Pacific Coast League. For which team?

a. L.A. Angels

b. Oakland Oaks

c. Portland Beavers

d. San Francisco Seals

7. Justin Verlander's spectacular 2011 campaign featured a 24-5 record and the ERA title (2.40). Who was the last previous starting pitcher to win the AL MVP Award?

a. Roger Clemens

b. Dennis Eckersley

c. Rollie Fingers

d. Bob Gibson

8. Verlander was unloaded by Detroit at the end of 2017. He promptly won a World Series with Houston. Who did he present with a wedding ring soon after?

a. Jennifer Aniston

b. Mila Kunis

c. Charlize Theron

d. Kate Upton

9. Hal Newhouser's teammate Dizzy Trout was another Detroit pitcher held out of WWII action. What was his issue?

a. Dizziness

b. High blood pressure

c. Pigeon toes

d. Hearing and sight impairments

10. What story did Dizzy Trout create to explain his nickname?

a. He crashed into an outfield wall thinking it was an awning.

b. He made hitters dizzy with his variety of tricky pitches.

c. He fell in love hard and often during his career.

d. He fell over first base trying to stretch a single.

11. Frank Lary was called "a workhorse" with a wild fastball from 1954 to 1964. He lorded it over one other team that was mostly winning at the time. Which?

a. Baltimore Orioles

b. Boston Red Sox

c. Cleveland Indians

d. New York Yankees

12. When Schoolboy Rowe set the baseball world on its ear with 16 straight wins in 1934, which team finally brought him crashing back to Earth?

a. Chicago White Sox

b. Philadelphia A's

c. St. Louis Cards

d. Washington Senators

13. Jim Bunning was an effective Detroit starter for nine seasons starting in 1955. What did he become after baseball?

a. Detroit mayor

b. Helicopter pilot

c. Hospital volunteer

d. U.S. Senator

14. Bunning was the only pitcher to ever strike out a specific Boston batter three times in one game. Who was the Beantowner?

a. Gator Greenwell

b. George Scott

c. Carl Yastrzemski

d. Ted Williams

15. One person credited with turning Denny McLain into a more fearsome pitcher was pitching coach Johnny Sain. Which pitch did he help Denny develop?

    a. Curve
    b. Forkball
    c. Knuckler
    d. Slider

16. McLain was controversial, but he indirectly helped Pepsi's marketing efforts. How many bottles of the sweet stuff did Denny polish off per day?

    a. 6
    b. 12
    c. 18
    d. 24

17. George Mullin took the mound for the Tigers from 1902 to 1913. What was the team record he set for most innings in 1904?

    a. 330
    b. 351.2
    c. 382.1
    d. 396

18. How did Mullin decide to celebrate his 32nd birthday?

    a. He invited all Tiger fans to his restaurant for free.
    b. He shut out the Cleveland Naps while hitting for the cycle.
    c. He stayed out all night and missed his start.
    d. He threw his only no-hitter.

19. While Hooks Dauss won more games than any Tigers pitcher (223), he also lost more than any other. How many?

    a. 156
    b. 177
    c. 182
    d. 192

20. Mickey Tettleton got on base and hit for power as the Detroit catcher in the early '90s. Which famous Oklahoman was he named after?

    a. Callaway
    b. Cochrane
    c. Mantle
    d. Mouse

QUIZ ANSWERS

1. D - His third straight MVP (AL)

2. A - True

3. C - Paul Richards

4. A - Harry Coveleski

5. B - Tommy Bridges

6. C - Portland Beavers

7. A - Roger Clemens

8. D - Kate Upton

9. D – Hearing and sight impairment

10. A - He crashed into an outfield wall thinking it was an awning.

11. D - New York Yankees

12. B - Philadelphia A's

13. D - U.S. Senator

14. D - Ted Williams

15. D - Slider

16. D - 24

17. C - 382.1

18. D - He threw his only no-hitter.

19. C - 182

20. C – Mantle

DID YOU KNOW?

1. Catcher "Pudge" Rodríguez won three Gold Glove awards with Detroit. Iván won the 2003 World Series with the Marlins but came up short in 2006 with Detroit.

2. During his lengthy career with six teams, in particular Texas, Pudge had the best caught-stealing percentage of any backstopper at 45.68%.

3. Lance Parrish was a big "raw" catcher when he started, but Bill Freehan taught him the position. Lance promptly made six All-Star teams and won three Gold Gloves in 10 years with the Tigers.

4. "The Big Wheel" Parrish clobbered 212 dingers with the Tigers and was the cleanup man in the 1984 Series for the winning Tigers.

5. In 1934 and 1935, Mickey Cochrane both managed and played behind the plate for the Tigers, leading them to back-to-back pennants and their first World Series win in '35.

6. Cochrane was literally almost killed by a beaning in 1937, ending his career. Yet he remains one of the three or four most vital Tigers ever in terms of winning.

7. Catcher Bill Freehan is considered "the heart" of the victorious 1968 Tigers, even though Denny McLain edged him in the AL MVP vote.

8. Overall, Freehan received MVP votes in six different years, and he finished in the Top 10 three times.

9. Called the best AL catcher for a decade (1963-1972), Freehan could do it all: handle pitchers, block the plate, and throw out runners. "It's a team thing and baseball is a team sport. But a lot of great players have never had the chance to play in a World Series, so it's the greatest thrill," Bill concluded.

10. Henry Franklin "Pig" House caught for Detroit in the '50s and 1961. He signed out of an Alabama high school in 1948 for one of the biggest bonuses at the time: $75,000 and two cars.

CHAPTER 9:

ODDS & ENDS

QUIZ TIME!

1. Comerica Park's management normally offers up new food treats every spring. As of 2019, who was the executive chef in charge?

   a. James Beard
   b. Chris Gerard
   c. Anthony Lombardo
   d. Mark Szubeczak

2. Guernsey Farms provides the Comerica Park ice cream delights. Which is the special Tigers flavor?

   a. Detroit Grand Slam
   b. Double Steal Double Choco
   c. Tasty Tiger Treat
   d. Tiger Tail Scream

3. A regular-season Tigers game uses a lot of baseballs, including batting practice and in the bullpen. How many?

a. 10 dozen

b. 15 dozen

c. 21 dozen

d. 25 dozen

4. Comerica opened in 2000 and hosted the All-Star Game in 2005. How much did the park cost to build?

a. $180 million

b. $250 million

c. $280 million

d. $300 million

5. The outfield fences in Comerica Park are all eight feet high, except for right-center field. How tall are they there?

a. 9 feet

b. 10 feet

c. 11 feet

d. 15 feet

6. The new home of the Detroit Lions is located just next to Comerica Park. What's its name?

a. Chrysler Field

b. Ford Field

c. Motown Arena

d. Michigan Coliseum

7. Comerica Inc. negotiated the naming rights to the park for 30 years. What business are they in?

a. Financial services

b. Food & beverage

c. Health care

d. Insurance

8. In 2005, Comerica's old bullpens were replaced by bleachers to create 9,500 new seats.

a. True

b. False

9. Where are Comerica's "new" bullpens now located?

a. Along the first base line

b. Along the third base line

c. Behind home plate

d. Beyond the outfield fences

10. What happens in the park when a Tiger hits a home run?

a. A Model-T Ford races along the outfield fence

b. Numerous lasers flash into the night sky

c. The two tigers atop the scoreboard jump up and down

d. The two tigers atop the scoreboard roar

11. Besides travel guides, which Fodor's publication includes a description of Comerica Park?

a. Fodor's Baseball Lover's Guide

b. Fodor's Baseball Vacations

c. Fodor's Freeway Friend

d. Fodor's Sports Spectacles

12. A walk-off home run by a Detroit slugger guaranteed the Tigers a trip to the 2006 World Series. Who was he?

a. Miguel Cabrera

b. Jason Grilli

c. Magglio Ordonez

d. Marcus Thames

13. On July 31, 2011, Carlos Guillén took Angels pitcher Jered Weaver deep and then stared him down. Weaver retaliated by tossing at Alex Avila's head and was ejected. Tigers win!

a. True

b. False

14. In a game on June 30, 2014, to mark the 30th anniversary of the 1984 championship, Detroit entered the bottom of the 9th trailing, 4-1. Who hit the walk-off shot to seal the 5-4 comeback?

a. Rajai Davis

b. Buck Farmer

c. Torii Hunter

d. Melvin Mercedes

15. Detroit bombed Boston in the second game of 2012 behind two Migeul Cabrera dingers. Who was the other slugger trying to make an impression as a new Tiger who also went deep twice?

a. Andy Dirks

b. Prince Fielder

c. Austin Jackson

d. Delmon Young

16. As of 2010, Detroit owner Michael Ilitch's net worth was calculated at $1.7 billion. What was the market value of the Tiger franchise?

a. $320 million
b. $355 million
c. $375 million
d. $415 million

17. In the same year, Detroit decided to get rid of $32.5 million of "underperforming" salaries. Which of the following players was NOT included in the house cleaning?

a. Jeremy Bonderman
b. Johnny Damon
c. Justin Verlander
d. Dontrelle Willis

18. What other Detroit team does Ilitch also own?

a. Lions
b. Pistons
c. Red Wings
d. Vipers

19. Which of the following is NOT one of Detroit's major corporate sponsors?

a. Chevrolet
b. Little Caesars
c. Microsoft
d. Miller Coors

20. What's the font of the stylized "D" on Detroit's uniforms?

a. Old English D
b. Old German D
c. Old Latin D
d. Old Lebanese D

QUIZ ANSWERS

1. D - Mark Szubeczak

2. A - Detroit Grand Slam

3. C - 21 dozen (252 balls)

4. D - $300 million

5. C - 11 feet

6. B - Ford Field

7. A - Financial Services

8. B - False / to create 950 new seats

9. D - Beyond the outfield fences

10. D - The two tigers atop the scoreboard roar.

11. B - Fodor's Baseball Vacations

12. C - Magglio Ordonez

13. A - True

14. A - Rajai Davis

15. B - Prince Fielder

16. C - $375 million

17. C - Justin Verlander

18. C - Red Wings

19. C - Microsoft

20. A - Old English D

DID YOU KNOW?

1. In 1938, Hank Greenberg hit 58 homers, a single-season Tigers record. "Big Daddy" Cecil Fielder did his best in 1990, ending up with 51.

2. Dick McAuliffe played in 151 Detroit games in 1968 and had 658 plate appearances without grounding into a single double play. In 1967, he played in 153 games but unfortunately was doubled up twice in 675 plate appearances.

3. Before Comerica, old Tiger Stadium was situated at Michigan and Trumbull Avenue. The team played at "the corner" from 1901 to 2000.

4. Long-time Tigers broadcaster Ernie Harwell once quipped: "Opening Day in Detroit is an event. It's New Year's, Easter, and Christmas all rolled into one unique afternoon."

5. Norman Dalton Cash walked away with the 1961 batting title after a sizzling .361 BA. In the following 12 Detroit seasons, he never again hit over .283.

6. In Mark Fidrych's rookie year, he barely made the roster and didn't make his first start till May 15, 1976. He then spun off nine wins in 10 starts, including two 11-inning complete games, and won the AL Rookie of the Year Award.

7. Twenty-one-year-old rookie Jon Warden was responsible for three wins in nine straight victories to start 1968 after Detroit lost its opening game to Boston. Warden was then drafted by the expansion Royals, hurt his arm, and was out of baseball.

8. In the 1901 and 1902 seasons, Detroit wasn't allowed to play ball on Sundays due to the city's "Blue Laws." Owner James Burns built a stadium on his own property so Sunday games could go ahead.

9. Hank Greenberg was busy winning MVPs in 1935 and 1940. He was then drafted by the Army but discharged two days before Japan bombed Pearl Harbor. Hank re-enlisted in the U.S. Air Force.

10. Elden Auker, a submarine-style pitcher in the 1930s, handed the Tigers flag from the old stadium flagpole to a 1999 Detroit tri-captain. He wrote all about it in "Sleeper Cars and Flannel Uniforms."

CHAPTER 10:

WHO'S ON FIRST?

QUIZ TIME!

1. In a long line of slugging Tiger first basemen, who came from Japan as a free agent to light the Detroit house on fire in 1990?

   a. Miguel Cabrera
   b. Cecil Fielder
   c. Prince Fielder
   d. Victor Martínez

2. Which Tigers first baseman received MVP votes in nine of the 10 years from 1937 through 1946, but never won the award?

   a. Hank Greenberg
   b. Harry Heilmann
   c. Claude Rossman
   d. Rudy York

3. To make room for Rudy York's dynamic bat, who did Detroit move to the outfield?

a. Pete Fox

b. Hank Greenberg

c. Barney McCoskey

d. Tuck Stainback

4. Pundits say the best trade in franchise history was acquiring Norm Cash from the Indians for Steve Demeter. Cash ended up blasting 373 homers for Detroit, second only to whom?

a. Miguel Cabrera

b. Willie Horton

c. Al Kaline

d. Hank Greenberg

5. Who played more games at first for Detroit than any other player?

a. Lu Blue

b. Miguel Cabrera

c. Norm Cash

d. Harry Heilmann

6. Which Detroit first baseman won the Triple Crown in 2012 for the first time since 1967?

a. Joaquín Benoit

b. Miguel Cabrera

c. Victor Martínez

d. Drew Smyly

7. Even Giants slugger Barry Bonds said of Cabrera: "He's the best. By far. Without a doubt. The absolute best." What country does "Miggy" come from?

a. Cuba

b. Dominican Republic

c. Puerto Rico

d. Venezuela

8. In how many seasons has Cabrera hit more than 30 homers?

a. 6

b. 8

c. 10

d. 12

9. The original "Hammerin' Hank," Greenberg was an RBI machine. How many homers and RBIs do projections say he lost due to 4.5 years of WW2 military service?

a. 150/500

b. 160/510

c. 180/550

d. 200/585

10. Maybe Cabrera can still pass Hank, but at the moment, the latter is the greatest right-handed power hitter in Tigers history. What was Greenberg's career slugging percentage?

a. .568

b. .595

c. .605

d. .624

11. Harry Heilmann was the Tigers' first baseman for more than 13 years and a Detroit broadcaster for 17. What was his nickname?

a. Handsome
b. Hellboy
c. Hippo
d. Slug

12. When Heilmann started as a Tiger broadcaster in 1934, who was his principal rival that could cover Detroit games exclusively in the city?

a. Ernie Harwell
b. George Kell
c. Van Patrick
d. Ty Tyson

13. Heilmann was elected to the Hall of Fame after he died of lung cancer in July 1951. What percentage of the vote did he receive?

a. 80
b. 83.25
c. 86.75
d. 92.5

14. Lu Blue grew up in D.C., a Washington Senators fan. Why did his parents not want him to play ball?

a. They thought he should become a teacher.
b. They thought it was a boring sport.
c. They thought it was an exclusive sport.
d. They thought it was a waste of time.

15. In 1921, Blue was installed as the regular Tiger first baseman. Who was the manager at that time?

    a. Ty Cobb
    b. Mickey Cochrane
    c. Bucky Harris
    d. George Stallings

16. In 1923, Luzerne Blue was knocked out after being hit in the head by a ball in fielding practice. What happened next?

    a. He asked to be traded.
    b. He hit a single in his first at-bat but could barely make it to first.
    c. He hit a home run in his first at-bat but passed out again.
    d. He went to the hospital and returned as a pinch hitter.

17. Blue had a falling out with his 1927 Detroit manager, George Moriarty. He was soon traded and became a star for his new team. Which?

    a. Brooklyn Dodgers
    b. Chicago Cubs
    c. N.Y. Yankees
    d. St. Louis Browns

18. Rick Leach was drafted in 1979 to play first for Detroit. Where was he a college football star?

    a. Michigan State
    b. Notre Dame

c. Ohio State

d. University of Michigan

19. Leach received a $150,000 signing bonus to play for Detroit. Which pro football team did he pass up in 1979 to play baseball?

a. Denver Broncos

b. Detroit Lions

c. New England Patriots

d. Seattle Seahawks

20. As a 12-year-old, Prince Fielder hit a shot into the upper deck of Tiger Stadium. Which coach was tossing batting practice at the time?

a. Buddy Bell

b. Terry Francona

c. Phil Garner

d. Larry Parrish

QUIZ ANSWERS

1. B - Cecil Fielder

2. D - Rudy York

3. B - Hank Greenberg

4. C - Al Kaline

5. C - Norm Cash

6. B - Miguel Cabrera

7. D - Venezuela

8. C - 10

9. C - 180 / 550

10. C - .605

11. D - Slug

12. D - Ty Tyson

13. C - 86.75

14. D - They thought it was a waste of time.

15. A - Ty Cobb

16. B - He hit a single in his first at-bat, but could barely make it to first.

17. D - St. Louis Browns

18. D - University of Michigan

19. A - Denver Broncos

20. B - Terry Francona

DID YOU KNOW?

1. On September 25, 2007, Prince Fielder became the youngest player ever to hit 50 homers in a season, joining his estranged father, Cecil, in the club.

2. Prince Fielder had to end his career due to his second neck surgery. All told, he had 319 dingers, the exact same number as his dad.

3. When the Prince arrived in Detroit in 2012, he earned a rather princely deal, raking in $214 million in a nine-year deal. That broke Cabrera's previous record, an eight-year deal for $152 million.

4. When first baseman Claude Rossman was sold to Detroit by the Cleveland Naps, he teamed with Ty Cobb, Sam Crawford and manager Hughie Jennings to haul in consecutive AL pennants in 1907 and 1908.

5. Rossman typically batted behind Cobb. His ability to lay down expert bunts often allowed Ty to streak from first to third without stopping.

6. In 2002, Detroit acquired Carlos Peña in a three-team deal allowing Randall Simon, the first baseman at the time, to move immediately into the DH spot to replace injured Dmitri Young.

7. Darrell Evans played first and DH for Detroit in their historic 1984 campaign. Evans was called "the most

underrated player in baseball history" by historian Bill James.

8. Darrell's dad passed away from cancer in July of '84. Evans said his greatest career disappointment was his father not seeing him play in the World Series.

9. From Tennessee, Dale "Moose" Alexander was one of the AL's premier hitters as a Tiger from 1929 to 1932. Unfortunately, he suffered third-degree burns when being treated for his injured knee, effectively finishing his career.

10. Despite the burns, Alexander was able to continue to play and then manage in the minors for such outfits as the Sanford Lookouts, Selma Cloverleafs and Thomasville Tourists.

CHAPTER 11:

WHO'S GOT SECOND?

QUIZ TIME!

1. Born and raised on a Michigan farm, which Detroit second baseman got a tryout via word of mouth?

   a. Charlie Gehringer
   b. Omar Infante
   c. Dick McAuliffe
   d. Jerry Priddy

2. Charlie Gehringer played all of his 2,223 games for the Tigers and all but 15 at second.

   a. True
   b. False

3. Gehringer played 150 games in at least nine seasons and batted .316 or better in 10 of his 16 seasons with at least 100 games played. What nickname did he earn?

   a. The Automatic Man
   b. Charlie Consistency

c. Gehringer the Greatest

d. The Mechanical Man

4. Marveling at Gehringer`s results, an admirer once joked, "You wind him up in the spring, turn him loose, he hits .330 or .340, and you shut him off at the end of the season." Who said it?

a. Dizzy Dean

b. Lefty Gomez

c. Mel Harder

d. Red Ruffing

5. Lou Whitaker turned some 1,527 career double plays. How does that rank all-time among second basemen?

a. 1st

b. 3rd

c. 4th

d. 6th

6. Which of the following second basemen did NOT join Sweet Lou in the club of 1,000 runs, 1,000 RBIs, 2,000 hits and 200 homers?

a. Bobby Doerr

b. Rogers Hornsby

c. Nap Lajoie

d. Joe Morgan

7. Whitaker and Trammell spent 19 years together as a middle infield tandem. Which of the following duos spent the second highest number of years together?

a. Johnny Evers and Joe Tinker

b. Joe Morgan and Dave Concepcion

c. Jackie Robinson and Pee Wee Reese

d. Chase Utley and Jimmy Rollins

8. Ian Kinsler provided both abundant offense and defense at second for Detroit from 2014 to 2017. How many defensive runs did he save in that time?

a. 30

b. 40

c. 50

d. 60

9. As well as grabbing a Gold Glove in 2016, which music icon did Kinsler ultimately partner with in a bat company?

a. Drake

b. Lady Gaga

c. Barry White

d. Jack White

10. Plácido Polanco played four positive years at second in Detroit. Who did the Tigers trade away to snare Polanco?

a. Chad Gaudin

b. Matt Lawton

c. Arthur Rhodes

d. Ugueth Urbina

11. Polanco quickly became a key Tiger and helped the squad slide into the 2006 World Series. How many consecutive losing seasons had Detroit endured up to that year?

a. 8

b. 10

c. 12

d. 13

12. Dick McAuliffe was Detroit's man at second in their run to the '68 Series. How many runs did he score that year?

a. 80

b. 87

c. 95

d. 101

13. McAuliffe finished 7th in the AL MVP vote in 1968. Which of the following Tigers did NOT finish ahead of him in that year's vote?

a. Gates Brown

b. Bill Freehan

c. Willie Horton

d. Denny McLain

14. In 2004, Omar Infante lost his chance at the shortstop spot when Detroit acquired Carlos Guillén. However, he stepped in at second when the regular went down injured. Who was he?

a. José Ascanio

b. Will Ohman

c. Ramón Santiago

d. Fernando Viña

15. Although Damion Easley hit for the cycle with Detroit in 2001, he was deemed expendable in 2003 by new manager Alan Trammell. How much salary did the Tigers eat by unloading him?

    a. $10 million
    b. $12.2 million
    c. $14.3 million
    d. $15.1 million

16. Frank Bolling played second for Detroit from 1954 to 1961. What was the name of his older brother, a big-league shortstop?

    a. Mark
    b. Matt
    c. Michael
    d. Milton

17. When Frank's brother joined Detroit in 1958, the Bolling boys became one of only four pairs of brothers in history to play the middle infield together. What's another name for this combo?

    a. The dynamic duo
    b. The keystone combination
    c. The keystone cops
    d. The turn-two tandem

18. Jerry Priddy played second for Detroit from 1950 to 1953. Which famous Yankee shortstop was he paired with in the minors?

a. Frank Crosetti

b. Derek Jeter

c. Roger Peckinpaugh

d. Phil Rizzuto

19. As a member of the Washington Senators, Priddy inspired a future MLB star at a clinic for African-American kids. Who was he?

a. Hank Aaron

b. Willie Mays

c. Frank Robinson

d. Maury Wills

20. Unfortunately, after his career, Priddy was arrested and spent nine months in prison. What was his crime?

a. Domestic violence

b. Extortion

c. Jaywalking

d. Selling corked bats

QUIZ ANSWERS

1. A - Charlie Gehringer

2. A - True

3. D - The Mechanical Man

4. B - Lefty Gomez

5. C - 4th

6. C - Nap Lajoie

7. D - Chase Utley and Jimmy Rollins

8. B - 40

9. D - Jack White

10. D - Ugueth Urbina

11. C - 12

12. C - 95

13. A - Gates Brown

14. D - Fernando Viña

15. C - $14.3 million

16. D - Milton

17. B - The keystone combination

18. D - Phil Rizzuto

19. D - Maury Wills

20. B - Extortion

DID YOU KNOW?

1. Edward Joseph Mayo manned second for Detroit during their pennant chases from 1944 to 1947. You can choose whichever of his nicknames you like better: "Hotshot" or "Steady Eddie."

2. Entering the 1945 season, writers were skeptical of Detroit's middle infield with Mayo and Skeeter Webb at shortstop, both 35 years old. They ended up winning the World Series, with Mayo MVP runner-up.

3. Germany Schaefer was at second for Detroit in the early 1900s. Known as a trickster, he'd take off from first, trying to draw a throw so his man could score from third. If he didn't, he'd "steal" first going back.

4. Schaefer's ability to "steal first" is detailed in Lawrence Ritter's book, "The Glory of Their Times", as recalled by teammate Davy Jones.

5. As a result of Schaefer's knack for confusing the opponents (and the umps), an MLB rule was passed preventing runners from "reverse stealing" or "making a travesty of the game."

6. "Kid" Gleason, known for his short stature and abundant energy, played second in Detroit from 1901 to 1902. He's one of a small group of men to play pro ball in four decades.

7. From New Jersey, Jake Wood was originally given credit as being the first African-American player developed by the Tigers system. Pitcher Jim Proctor was later given the nod; Proctor debuted in 1959.

8. When Detroit picked up veteran second baseman Jerry Lumpe in 1964, Jake Wood became a utility player.

9. In 2004, Carlos Guillén had a career year after joining Detroit from Seattle: 97 RBIs, 97 runs, 37 doubles and a .318 BA.

10. In 2006, Carlos became the first player in modern MLB history to raise his average in six straight seasons. He also led the AL in errors with 28 after moving back to shortstop in 2006.

CHAPTER 12:

WHO'S AT THE HOT CORNER?

QUIZ TIME!

1. "Bonus Baby" Steve Boros signed for $25,000 to play with Detroit in 1957. How many teams were bidding for him at the time?

   a. 8
   b. 10
   c. 12
   d. 14

2. While Boros played with Detroit, he expressed to reporters his love of literature and desire to become a professor of the subject.

   a. True
   b. False

3. Later, as manager of the San Jose Bees, Boros advocated the stolen base as an attacking component. What was his team's modern minor league set for stolen bags in a season?

a. 322

b. 337

c. 352

d. 371

4. Who was the franchise's original third baseman when Detroit took off in 1901?

   a. Jimmy Barrett

   b. Doc Casey

   c. Kid Elberfeld

   d. Roscoe Miller

5. Since both the AL and NL were competing for the same players then, which club's contract did Doc Casey "jump" to get to the Tigers?

   a. Boston Americans

   b. Brooklyn Superbas

   c. Chicago White Stockings

   d. Cleveland Blues

6. After the Tigers, Doc jumped again to the Cubs. He was part of the famous infield: "Tinkers to Evers to _____!" Who's missing?

   a. Chance

   b. Fortune

   c. Luck

   d. Waddell

7. After Casey's career wound down, he returned to Detroit to practice dentistry and the best place to talk baseball in the winter. What was it?

a. A bar

b. A coffee shop

c. A drug store

d. A luncheonette

8. Tom Brookens was the mainstay at the Detroit hot corner during the 1980s. Which of the following did NOT replace him at some point?

a. Darnell Coles

b. Barbaro Garbey

c. John Hiller

d. Ray Knight

9. Tom had a twin brother who played in the Tigers farm system but never made it to the big leagues. What was his name?

a. Ted

b. Terry

c. Tim

d. Trot

10. After the 1988 season, Tom Brookens was traded to the Yankees for another aging player, Charles Hudson. How many more games did Hudson last in the majors?

a. 13

b. 18

c. 25

d. 35

11. Bob "Ducky" Jones took over for a fielding whiz at third for Detroit in 1919. Who was the other character?

a. Babe Ellison

b. Ira Flagstead

c. Ossie Vitt

d. Ralph Young

12. After the 1925 season, Jones was traded along with five others for one promising player, Jack Warner, in the Pacific Coast League. What was Warner's team?

a. L.A. Angels

b. Portland Beavers

c. Seattle Indians

d. Vernon Tigers

13. Playing third and slugging for Detroit in 1999 and 2000, Dean Palmer had two seasons with more than 100 RBIs. He also had a fair number of strikeouts. How many?

a. 199

b. 239

c. 299

d. 339

14. Bill Coughlin served as Tiger captain and fireplug on the 1907 and 1908 World Series teams that lost to the Cubs. What was his nickname?

a. Barnstormin' Bill

b. Buffalo Bill

c. Rowdy Bill

d. Crazy Coughlin

15. In Game 2 of the 1907 World Series, Coughlin pulled off quite a trick. What was it?

a. Delayed steal

b. Hidden ball

c. Potato play

d. Skunk in the outfield

16. George Moriarty took over at third after Coughlin headed for the Senators. Besides being a Tigers manager, what else did George do in life?

a. Barge operator

b. Construction company owner

c. Major league umpire

d. News correspondent

17. Ossie Vitt handled the Detroit hot corner in 1916, and also survived a public spat with Ty Cobb. What did Vitt accuse Cobb of?

a. Caring only about money

b. Caring only for his own stats

c. Refusing to bunt his teammate over

d. Refusing to clean his shoes before entering the locker room

18. Vitt went on to manage the Cleveland Indians from 1938 to 1940. What was the Cleveland team called during Vitt's tenure?

a. Clowns

b. Crybabies

c. Inept Indians

d. Plate Crowders

19. George Moriarty was a key player at third as Detroit went for a third straight pennant in 1909. What ability was he known for?

   a. Bunting
   b. Slick fielding
   c. Stealing home
   d. Throwing off balance

20. Marty McManus spent parts of five seasons with Detroit before bussing off to Boston in 1931. Who was the catcher Detroit got in return that didn't pan out?

   a. Al Bool
   b. Jack Crouch
   c. Spud Davis
   d. Muddy Ruel

QUIZ ANSWERS

1. D - 14

2. A - True

3. D - 371

4. B - Doc Casey

5. B - Brooklyn Superbas

6. A - Chance

7. C - a drug store

8. C - John Hiller

9. C - Tim

10. B - 18

11. C - Ossie Vitt

12. D - Vernon Tigers

13. C - 299

14. C - Rowdy Bill

15. B - Hidden ball

16. C - Major league umpire

17. B - Caring only for his own stats

18. B - Crybabies

19. C - Stealing home

20. D - Muddy Ruel

DID YOU KNOW?

1. Since Marty McManus was often a holdout during his career, he was involved in an American Federation of Labor effort to unionize pro baseball, basketball, and football players in 1951.

2. Even though Eddie Yost's numbers had slipped with Washington in 1958, he gave Detroit two great seasons. He was often called "Walking Man" for obvious reasons.

3. Aurélio Rodríguez was a fan favorite with a powerful arm who played more games at third than any other Tiger. His light-hitting stats were more common of '70s-era shortstops.

4. Don Wert was another fine-fielding third basemen for Detroit but he was overshadowed by the greatness of the Orioles' Brooks Robinson.

5. Wert clocked the game-winning RBI as the Tigers clinched the '68 pennant. Don went on to bat a dismal .118 in the World Series against the Cards.

6. Marv Owen owned the hot corner in 1934 when the Tigers put together an infield called the "Battalion of Death," featuring Hank Greenberg, Charlie Gehringer, and Billy Rogell.

7. Owen managed to hit only .061 in two World Series, but his fight with the Cards' Joe "Ducky" Medwick turned into a riot and led to the latter's ejection.

8. Pinky Higgins had enough in the tank to help Detroit into the 1940 World Series and even got some MVP votes in 1944. He was also later blamed as the Red Sox manager for the team's slowness to integrate.

9. Brandon Inge was booed for fanning later in his career but was the first player after Dean Palmer in 1999 to hold the third base job for more than a year.

10. Travis Fryman gave the Tigers three All-Star years at third. He was often unfairly cast in Alan Trammell's shadow as Detroit battled to win in the 1990s.

CHAPTER 13:

WHO'S AT SHORT?

QUIZ TIME!

1. Terrific Tigers shortstop Alan Trammell joined an elite club by playing 20 years for the Detroit Tigers. How many other players did the same?

   a. 2
   b. 3
   c. 4
   d. 6

2. In how many of those years did Trammell hit .300 or better?

   a. 4
   b. 6
   c. 7
   d. 9

3. The fact that Trammel somehow did not win the 1987 AL MVP is still tough for Tigers fans to swallow. Who won the award?

a. George Bell

b. Dwight Evans

c. Don Mattingly

d. Kirby Puckett

4. Which of the following was NOT one of Trammell's main idols growing up?

a. Roberto Clemente

b. Charlie Hough

c. Al Kaline

5. In 1912, Donie Bush had almost as many walks as hits. How many walks did he have?

a. 107

b. 117

c. 125

d. 136

6. The 5-foot-6 switch-hitter Bush bashed all of nine homers in his career. How many were inside-the-park jobs?

a. 5

b. 6

c. 7

d. 8

7. In the same summer (1953) that Al Kaline signed with Detroit out of high school, what did Harvey Kuenn accomplish?

a. Batting champion

b. MVP

c. Rookie of the Year

d. Triple Crown

8. Which university was Kuenn recruited from in 1952?

   a. Michigan

   b. Minnesota

   c. North Dakota

   d. Wisconsin

9. In 1954, Kuenn's second complete year with Detroit, how many times did he strike out in 656 at-bats?

   a. 10

   b. 13

   c. 17

   d. 21

10. Billy Rogell played short and was an integral part of the "Battalion of Death" infield configuration. What was his nickname?

    a. Billy Burn

    b. Fire Chief

    c. Fire Marshall

    d. Rapid Fire Rogell

11. Marv Owen once said about Rogell's smoothness with the glove: "He's the only player I ever knew who could catch a bad ____." What's missing?

    a. ball

    b. bounce

    c. hit

    d. hop

12. In 1934, without letting the media or the opposing Cardinals know, Rogell played the World Series with a broken bone and managed 8 hits and 4 RBI in seven games. What was busted?

    a. ankle
    b. finger
    c. rib
    d. toe

13. Carlos Guillén helped Detroit at short from 2004 until he retired in 2011. Who originally signed him?

    a. Atlanta
    b. Florida
    c. Houston
    d. Seattle

14. Born in Connecticut, the "Constitution State," where did Detroit shortstop Dick McAuliffe go to high school?

    a. Farmington
    b. Glastonbury
    c. West Hartford
    d. Windsor

15. In the 1961 and 1962 seasons, McAuliffe was moved between second and short for Detroit. When he finally became a regular in 1963, who was the odd man out?

    a. Chico Fernández
    b. Whitey Herzog
    c. Bubba Morton
    d. Gus Triandos

16. Cuban Jose Iglesias made it to the big leagues by defecting while his junior national team played in Canada. He was signed first by the Red Sox as an international free agent in 2009.

    a. True
    b. False

17. In 2014, shortstop Ramón Santiago became the only player in MLB history to hit a walk-off grand slam in his last career at-bat. Against whom?

    a. Philadelphia
    b. Pittsburgh
    c. Texas
    d. Toronto

18. In 2004, Jhonny Peralta was named the International League's MVP for a Cleveland affiliate before making his way to Detroit. Which minor league team did he play for?

    a. Buffalo Bisons
    b. Lehigh Valley IronPigs
    c. Pawtucket Red Sox
    d. Toledo Mud Hens

19. While a Tiger in 2013, Peralta served a suspension for his part in the Biogenesis performance-enhancing drug scandal. How many games did he miss at short?

    a. 25
    b. 50
    c. 60
    d. 75

20. Tom Veryzer was drafted by Detroit to play short in 1971. His older brother James was drafted in 1967. By which team?

    a. Kansas City A's

    b. Minnesota Twins

    c. Oakland A's

    d. San Francisco Giants

QUIZ ANSWERS

1. A - 2

2. C - 7

3. A - George Bell

4. B - Charlie Hough

5. B - 117

6. C - 7

7. C - Rookie of the Year

8. D - Wisconsin

9. B - 13

10. B - Fire Chief

11. D - hop

12. A - ankle

13. C - Houston

14. A - Farmington

15. A - Chico Fernández

16. A - True

17. B - Pittsburgh

18. A - Buffalo Bisons

19. B - 50

20. A - Kansas City A's

DID YOU KNOW?

1. Ed Brinkman played in high school alongside the illustrious Pete Rose. At one point, coach "Pappy" Nohr described Rose as "a good ballplayer, not a Brinkman."

2. Rose later joked about the $75,000 bonus the Senators shelled out in 1961 for Brinkman. Ed's bonus was apparently brought in an armored car, while Rose cashed his "at the corner store."

3. Emory "Topper" Rigney had one of the best range factors of all shortstops in his era. In 1923, Rigney suffered from a hip problem until doctors discovered he had several infected molars.

4. Rigney's .410 on-base percentage in 1924 is the highest ever for a Tiger shortstop. Take care of your teeth!

5. Ray Oyler played short for the Tigers in the 1968 season. He's known for having the lowest batting average of any position player with at least 1,000 at-bats in modern MLB history.

6. After Oyler went "0-for-August," Tiger coach Mayo Smith gambled by bringing in outfielder Mickey Stanley to play short in the '68 World Series. Oyler did appear as a defensive replacement.

7. ESPN later rated Smith's decision as one of the ten greatest coaching moves of the century.

8. Johnny Lipon didn't hit much but he forced Cleveland's Bob Feller to lose the shutout while pitching his third no-hitter. Lipon reached on an error, stole second, went to third on a wild pickoff throw, and scored on a sacrifice fly.

9. Kid Elberfeld, nicknamed "the Tabasco Kid" for his fiery temper, was once suspended for all of eight games after attacking ump Silk O'Loughlin in the early 1900s. Kid was removed by police.

10. Shortstop Eddie Lake was traded from Boston to Detroit for Rudy York in 1946. Lake then scored 108 runs for the Tigers while York helped Boston to its first AL pennant in 28 years.

CHAPTER 14:

THE OUTFIELD GANG

QUIZ TIME!

1. Bobby Veach patrolled Detroit's outfield from 1912 to 1923. Yet he still played in the shadows of three other Detroit Hall of Famers due to their 16 combined batting titles. Which of the following is NOT one of them?

   a. Ty Cobb
   b. Sam Crawford
   c. Harry Heilmann
   d. Davy Jones

2. Veach was born in Island, Kentucky, and started working alongside his dad as a coal miner at age 14. He claimed that he continued mining in the winters 'long after' he was earning money as a player."

   a. True
   b. False

3. The 1915 Tigers outfield, with Veach in left, Cobb in center, and Crawford in right, has been ranked as "the

greatest of all time" by one prominent baseball historian. Who was he?

a. Charles Alexander
b. Bill James
c. Roger Kahn
d. Mark Kurlansky

4. When Sam Crawford was growing up in Nebraska in 1898, he joined a traveling baseball team that went from town to town, challenging the locals. What mode of transport did they use?

a. Horse
b. Lumber wagon
c. River barge
d. Train

5. Crawford was offered $65 to play with the Chatham Reds in the 1899 Canadian League. What job did he quickly drop?

a. Barber's apprentice
b. Dishwasher
c. Shoeshine boy
d. Butcher

6. During a 1902 bidding war, Crawford signed with the NL Reds and the AL Tigers. In the end, a judge decided for the Tigers. What was the extra amount the Tigers paid the Reds?

a. $1,000
b. $3,000

c. $5,500

d. $10,000

7. As an 11-year-old boy, Harry Heilmann survived the 1906 San Francisco earthquake. What percent of the city's population was homeless and living in refugee camps afterward?

   a. 40%

   b. 50%

   c. 65%

   d. 75%

8. Heilmann was among the AL's batting leaders in almost every 1916 category. He was also famous off the field. For what?

   a. He acted as a museum educator.

   b. He participated in a danceathon.

   c. He saved a woman in the Detroit River.

   d. He volunteered at the local soup kitchen.

9. "Mr. Tiger" Al Kaline played most of his Detroit career in right field and was renowned for his cannon throwing arm. How many Gold Gloves did he win?

   a. 6

   b. 8

   c. 10

   d. 13

10. Kaline broke all kinds of records at a young age. His foot continued to bother him until finally an orthopedic

surgeon prescribed corrective shoes in 1965. The doc said, "Kaline has bordered on being a _____."

a. cripple

b. invalid

c. lunatic

d. monster

11. The man Kaline tried to catch: Ty Cobb. The Georgia Peach was elected to the Hall of Fame on his inaugural ballot with 98.2% of the vote. Who was the next player in time to get more?

a. George Brett

b. Ken Griffey, Jr.

c. Nolan Ryan

d. Tom Seaver

12. Cobb was later accused of racism, but he spoke favorably of blacks and was a famous philanthropist. Which biographer has been discredited for sensationalizing Cobb's story?

a. Charles Leerhsen

b. H.G. Salsinger

c. Al Stump

13. Hank Greenberg played in Detroit's outfield but originally liked first base. He was wooed by the Yankees who already had first baseman Lou Gehrig. For how much did Hank sign with Detroit in 1930?

a. $6,000

b. $9,000

c. $13,000

d. $20,000

14. One silly relief pitcher refused to walk Kirk Gibson with a base open. Gibby then blasted the winning shot in the 1984 Series. Who was the hapless New Yorker?

a. Goose Gossage

b. Ron Guidry

c. Phil Niekro

d. Mariano Rivera

15. Born in Arno, Virginia, in 1942, Willie Horton was the youngest of how many children in his family?

a. 11

b. 15

c. 18

d. 21

16. How old was Willie when he hit his first home run at Tiger Stadium?

a. 16 years

b. 18 years

c. 20 years

d. 22 years

17. Curtis Granderson proved to be an outstanding outfielder for Detroit. What award did he also win in 2016 for contributions to the community, especially the inner city?

a. Community Heroes Award

b. Detroit Community Development Award

c. Roberto Clemente Award

d. Spirit of Community Award

18. Granderson grew up a Braves fan. Which hometown team did he NOT like because its game interrupted his favorite program, "Saved by the Bell"?

a. Chicago Cubs

b. Chicago White Sox

c. New York Mets

d. New York Yankees

19. Cameron Maybin has had two stints in the Detroit outfield (2007 and 2016). How many other teams has he played for?

a. 5

b. 7

c. 8

d. 10

20. Mickey Stanley played his entire 12-year career for Detroit. He had speed, a strong arm, and the ability to take the perfect first step in center field to get a jump on balls. He twice led AL outfielders with a perfect 1.000 fielding percentage.

a. True

b. False

QUIZ ANSWERS

1. D - Davy Jones

2. A - Yes

3. B - Bill James

4. B - Lumber wagon

5. A - Barber's apprentice

6. B - $3,000

7. D - 75

8. C - He saved a woman in the Detroit River.

9. C - 10

10. A - cripple

11. D - Tom Seaver

12. C - Al Stump

13. B - $9,000 ($138K today)

14. A - Goose Gossage

15. D - 21

16. A - 16 years

17. C - Roberto Clemente Award

18. A - Chicago Cubs

19. B - 7

20. A - True

DID YOU KNOW?

1. Stanley did it all with the glove. With the bat, he was a bit less successful. After striking out against Nolan Ryan in his no-hitter, Stanley quipped, "Those were the best pitches I ever heard."

2. Born in Miami of Cuban descent, J.D. Martínez became the 18th major leaguer to bop four homers in a single game against the Dodgers in 2017. '

3. Austin Jackson blazed around the Detroit outfield from 2010 to 2014. In 1999, he was named the best 12-year-old player in the nation and, three years later, the best 15-year-old.

4. When Torii Hunter made the Junior Olympic Team, he couldn't afford the expenses. He wrote for help to the then-governor of Arkansas, Bill Clinton, who sent him a check for $500.

5. Chet Lemon was one of the best defensive center fielders in MLB for a decade and Detroit's starter in 1984. He was criticized for not standing during the anthem due to his beliefs as Jehovah's Witness.

6. Jim "The Silver Fox" Northrup had the versatility in the outfield to take over in center when Mayo Smith made his masterful Mickey move in the '68 Series.

7. Bobby Higginson was named "Tiger of The Year" by

baseball writers in 1997 and 2000 (along with ten other Detroit players also named on multiple occasions).

8. On September 21, 2013, Detroit staged a wild 7-6 comeback win over the White Sox, after trailing 6-0. Outfielder Andy Dirks had a key three-run blast as a pinch hitter.

9. Before becoming a Tiger, Brennan Boesch was on display for California coaches in 2004. He swung at three pitches, all homers, and his fate was sealed. He attended Cal-Berkeley and clocked one out on the first pitch he faced.

10. Gary Sheffield terrorized Tiger opponents in 2007 and 2008. "I can't imagine there's ever been a scarier hitter to face," gushed sportswriter Joe Posnanski.

CHAPTER 15:

THE HEATED RIVALRIES

QUIZ TIME!

1. Clearly, the biggest traditional Tiger rival is the Cleveland Indians. Who ranks second?

   a. Chicago White Sox

   b. Kansas City

   c. Minnesota

   d. New York Yankees

2. Between the two states involved, what other sports rivalry comes close in intensity?

   a. Detroit Pistons vs. Cleveland Cavs

   b. Detroit Lions vs. Cleveland Browns

   c. U. of Michigan vs. Ohio State

   d. Michigan State vs. Ohio Wesleyan

3. One of Detroit's earliest rivals beat the Tigers in their first two World Series encounters. Which team?

   a. Cleveland Naps

   b. Chicago Cubs

c. Chicago Fire

d. Milwaukee Brewers

4. Sometimes the fans want to rival the players. Which Tiger entered the stands in 1912 to quiet a fan abusing him?

a. Ty Cobb

b. Hooks Dauss

c. Baldy Lauden

d. Bun Troy

5. One reason for great rivalries is geographical distance. What's the distance between Cleveland and the Motor City, as the crow flies?

a. 60 miles

b. 75 miles

c. 90 miles

d. 125 miles

6. How long have Detroit and Cleveland competed in the same division?

a. 90 years

b. 100 years

c. 115 years

d. 125 years

7. Despite their storied rivalry, before the 2007 season, the Tigers and Indians had gone 67 years without finishing one and two in the standings.

a. True

b. False

8. The 2013 race seemed tight but, in fact, the Tigers outplayed Cleveland, 15 wins to 4. How many more runs did Detroit score than Cleveland that year in head-to-head games?

   a. 20
   b. 30
   c. 40
   d. 50

9. Major league expansion meant that Detroit inherited some new rivals. In what year were they placed in the AL East Division?

   a. 1957
   b. 1969
   c. 1972
   d. 1976

10. The Tigers took the field under fiery manager Billy Martin and beat the Red Sox to clinch the East title in 1972. Who was the surprising pitcher that year who went 10-3 and restricted all rivals?

    a. Joe Coleman
    b. Woodie Fryman
    c. Phil Meeler
    d. Bill Slayback

11. Martin didn't survive the 1973 season as he admittedly ordered his pitchers to get revenge on Cleveland hurler Gaylord Perry. What did Martin demand of his staff?

a. Bean the Indians

b. Deliberately delay the game

c. Intentionally scuff the ball

d. Throw spitters

12. In 1984, broadcasting bigwig John Fetzer sold the club for $53 million. To whom?

a. Howard Schultz/Starbucks

b. Phil Knight/Nike

c. Tom Monaghan/Domino's Pizza

d. Sam Walton/Walmart

13. National TV can help intensify rivalries. After getting off to a 9-0 start in 1984, which Tiger pitched a nationally televised no-hitter against the White Sox?

a. Juan Berenguer

b. Jack Morris

c. Dan Petry

d. Milt Wilcox

14. In Game 2 of the 1984 ALCS against the Royals, Johnny Grubb's double in the 11th polished off K.C. Who was the unlucky Royal closer that night?

a. Joe Beckwith

b. Bud Black

c. Charlie Liebrandt

d. Dan Quisenberry

15. To beat your rivals, you need runs. "The problem with John Wockenfuss getting on base is that it takes three

doubles to score him," one Tigers manager lamented. Who was he?

a. Sparky Anderson
b. Ron Gardenhire
c. Hughie Jennings
d. Jim Leyland

16. Ty Cobb's main rival wasn't another team, either as a player or manager. Which opponent turned into a bigger story than Ty in 1919?

a. Joe Dempsey
b. Duffy Lewis
c. Ivy Olson
d. Babe Ruth

17. Even though Larry Doby started with rival Cleveland in 1947, he later came home to Detroit. What was Larry the second African-American man ever in MLB to do?

a. Break the color barrier
b. Break the sound barrier with his bat
c. Hit homers in 10 straight games
d. Hit for the cycle three times in a season

18. How many letters – mostly in protest – did Cleveland owner Bill Veeck receive about signing Doby?

a. 5,000
b. 12,000
c. 20,000
d. 35,000

19. The 2015 Hall of Fame class included former Tigers' prospect, John Smoltz, but somehow Alan Trammell didn't make it. Which of the following was also NOT elected?

    a. Craig Biggio
    b. Randy Johnson
    c. Pedro Martínez
    d. Tim Raines

20. A good way to get your rivals riled up is a beaning. Detroit's Jeff Weaver drilled Chicago's Carlos Lee in 2000. At the end of the day, how many players from both teams were ejected?

    a. 7
    b. 9
    c. 11
    d. 16

QUIZ ANSWERS

1. A - Chicago White Sox

2. C - U. of Michigan vs. Ohio State

3. B - Cubs

4. A - Ty Cobb

5. C - 90 miles

6. C - 115 years

7. A - True

8. D - 50

9. B - 1969

10. B - Woodie Fryman

11. D - Throw spitters

12. C - Tom Monaghan / Domino's Pizza

13. B - Jack Morris

14. D - Dan Quisenberry

15. A - Sparky Anderson

16. D - Babe Ruth

17. A - Break the color barrier

18. C - 20,000

19. D - Tim Raines

20. C - 11

DID YOU KNOW?

1. In the aforementioned historic game, beanings happened again in the 9th inning. MLB later suspended 16 players, a new kind of baseball record.

2. Legendary manager Sparky Anderson wasn't worried about rivals in 1984 when the Tigers got so far ahead. "If we lose this thing, they're going to string me up on that flag pole in center field," he said of Detroiters.

3. Hard to believe that rivals would fix a game, but Ty Cobb and Tris Speaker were accused of just that in a Detroit-Cleveland matchup. Manager Hughie Jennings finally said, "My slate has been clean baseball for 35 years."

4. Tigers great Kirk Gibson kept it simple: "Our biggest challenge is we played Boston, Cleveland, the White Sox, and Cleveland again."

5. After playing for some minor league outfits like the Reading Pretzels, Bucky Harris got the nod as a manager in Detroit in 1929. He stressed the importance of not having rivals inside the same club: "There are only two things a manager needs to know: When to change pitchers and how to get along with your players."

6. During the 1980s, a strong rivalry developed between the Toronto Blue Jays and Detroit as they shared the same area code in the AL East. That rivalry cooled off a bit in 1998 when the Tigers moved over to the AL Central Division.

7. The AL Central Division is one of only two (of six total in MLB) in which every team has won at least one World Series. In fact, all five teams—Detroit, Chicago White Sox, Cleveland, K.C. Royals, and Minnesota—have won two.

8. When White Sox skipper Ozzie Guillén was "visually upset" that a retaliation pitch by Chicago's Jon Garland had failed, Detroit coach Andy Van Slyke smoothed things over saying that he'd have punched Guillén if that happened to him.

9. Baseball is all about history. Back in 1907 and 1908, interleague play meant only one thing: the World Series. The Tigers lost both those Series to the Cubs, but they bounced back in 1935 and 1945. The rivalry remains even at two apiece.

10. What do rivals really mean? Listen to all-time great Tiger announcer Ernie Harwell: "So much happened (in 1968) it was hard to keep up with everything. We had Denny McLain's thirty-one victories, Gates Brown's great pinch-hitting in the clutch, Tom Matchick's home run to beat Baltimore in the ninth inning, then Daryl Patterson striking out the side to beat them in the ninth. Excitement every day in the ballpark."

CONCLUSION

The great Tigers names roll off your tongue: Freehan, Greenberg, Gehringer, Gibson, Al Kaline, Morris, Sparky, Trammell, and the iconic Ty Cobb, the man who broke 90 MLB records.

Here you have it: an amazing collection of Tigers trivia, information, and statistics at your fingertips! Regardless of how you fared on the quizzes, we hope you found this book entertaining, enlightening and educational.

Ideally, you knew many of these details already but also learned a good deal more about the history of the Tigers, their players, coaches, managers, and some of the quirky stories surrounding the team, its history and its special stadium. If you got a little peek into the colorful details that make being a fan so much more enjoyable, then our mission was accomplished!

The good news is the trivia doesn't have to stop there. Spread the word. Challenge your fellow Tigers fans to see if they can do any better. Share some of the stories with the next generation to help them become Tigers supporters too.

If you are a big enough Detroit fan, consider creating your own quiz with some of the details you know weren't presented here. Then test your friends to see if they can match your knowledge.

The Tigers are one of baseball's most storied franchises with a long history, so many stretches of success, and a few that were a bit less successful. They've had glorious superstars, iconic moments, and hilarious tales... but most of all, they have wonderful, passionate fans. Thank you for being one of them. "Always a Tiger."